Table of Contents

EU Constitution: "Non" for Now—or Fore
The French Rejection in Historical Perspec.
The Constitution: Sowing the Seeds of Failure	3
Britain	6
France	8
Germany	10
Italy	11
East-Central Europe	13
Where will the EU go from here?	15

EU Constitution: "Non" for Now--or Forever?

Since voters in France and the Netherlands rejected the EU Constitution, European politics has been thrown into a period of turmoil and reflection. Consequently, we thought it would be useful to provide instructors and students with a quick and, under the circumstances, quite comprehensive discussion and analysis of causes and consequences of the May-June 2005 rejection of the Constitution.

What are the implications for EU institutions and agendas? How did domestic politics in each country shape citizen reactions to the Constitution—and what are the domestic political ramifications of the defeat? What comes next? Is this a temporary setback for the robust EU agenda of enlargement, economic integration, and greater geopolitical cohesion? Or has Europe stumbled badly, never to recover. Hence the subtitle of this supplement: "non" for now—or forever?

The following discussion is intended to clarify the issues involved in the constitutional debate and to provoke interesting and productive class debates as we all try to come to terms with this new critical juncture in European politics. As with so many key moments in the evolution of European politics, we begin with developments in France.

The French Rejection in Historical Perspective

Throughout the history of the EU, the French have been the guiding force in setting European agendas and defining critical moments in the evolution of the project of European integration. French citizen Jean Monnet was informally known as the father of Europe: he conceived the plan for the Coal and Steel Community (the forerunner of the EU). In the 1980s, another Frenchman, Jacques Delors, as president of the European Commission, provided the energy and vision to initiate the plan for Economic and Monetary Union that led to the creation of the euro. And so the French exerted their unique influence on the EU again in 2005, but in a very different way. In a referendum held on May 29, 2005, French voters rejected the Constitution by a wide margin. Their action precipitated the most intense crisis in the EU's 50-year history.

A first draft of the Treaty Establishing a Constitution for Europe was drawn up by the Convention on the Future of Europe. The Member States then convened an Intergovernmental Conference (IGC) in October 2003, taking the draft prepared by the Convention as their starting point. In June 2004, facing the prospect of a rancorous defeat, agreement was reached and in Rome in October 2004, the document was signed by all the member states.

By 2005, all that remained for it to become binding was ratification by member states. (EU regulations required that all 25 member states approve the treaty.) The ratification process was well underway when French voters went to the polls. Austria, Germany, Greece, Hungary, Italy, Latvia, Lithuania, Slovakia, and Slovenia had already approved the treaty by parliamentary vote, and Spain had approved it by referendum. No country had rejected it.
French president Jacques Chirac could have requested that the French parliament approve the treaty. Given that his party had a solid majority in parliament, approval would have been a foregone conclusion. However, Chirac instead sponsored a nationwide referendum to give France's approval a more dramatic character—and to enhance his own domestic and international standing.

By early 2005, it was clear that Chirac had committed a major blunder by choosing the route of a referendum. Despite the fact that all three major French governing parties—usually bitter opponents on most issues--officially supported the referendum, the Constitution was rejected by 55 percent of the French who turned out to vote. (In the section on France below, we analyze the multiple factors that produced the "non" vote.)

Three days after the French "non," Dutch voters rejected the treaty by a 62 percent majority—significantly larger than the French outcome. The Dutch government, presiding over a recession, was also unpopular. Many in the Netherlands feared that the new Constitution would reinforce the power of larger member states in the EU at the expense of the "smalls." There was also some Dutch anxiety that Europe might "harmonize" out of existence some of Dutch society's social liberalism (tolerance for soft drugs and euthanasia, for example). The Dutch were in the midst of a major crisis of conscience about immigration. The discovery that immigrants were not learning Dutch and resisting assimilation plus the assassinations of public figures who had taken strong positions on immigration had stimulated deep debate about past and future policies. Hence, it was a bad moment to ask the Dutch about Europe.

A devastating one-two blow, the resounding French and Dutch no votes provoked a huge European crisis. Jacques Chirac and Tony Blair engaged in a bitter public dispute involving the EU budget. Chirac called for Blair to accept the scaling down of an annual budget rebate that Britain has received from the EU since 1984 (to offset the great expense of the Common Agricultural Policy or CAP that accounts for more than 40 percent of the EU budget). Blair called for the reduction of agricultural subsidies—a hefty portion of which went to French farmers.

Acrimony between national leaders around major disagreements about the EU's future foretold difficult years to come. Clearly, the French "non" has helped precipitate a new moment of transition in European politics. What are the roots of that crisis, its character, and possible outcome? To explore these questions more deeply, we discuss developments at the level, first, of the European Union, and then turn to key countries affected by the crisis.

The Constitution: Sowing the Seeds of Failure

The European Convention was intended to bring the European Union closer to European peoples. It was designed, above all, to resolve the serious problems of popular disinterest and disenchantment. What a bitter irony that the "Treaty Establishing a Constitution for Europe" it produced would become a lightning rod for every perceived slight and every discontent about Europe—and about national politics, political elites, and economic problems as well.

The idea was to gather a broadly representative group of leaders and organizations, mandated to consult as widely as they could, to propose solutions to EU institutional problems tied to the Union's Central and Eastern European enlargement, to work on important unresolved policy matters (such as defense and foreign policy and key "justice and home affairs" issues such as immigration), and to re-codify the EU's existing legal and institutional foundations in ways that ordinary citizens could understand.

Valéry Giscard d'Estaing, the Convention president and former president of France, was a distinguished and intelligent politician, but too haughty, aristocratic, and old to communicate with Europe's newer generations. His assistants, Giuliano Amato and Jean-Luc de Haene, the former prime ministers of Italy and Belgium, respectively, were seasoned wheeler-dealers. Hence, the consultation was trapped in a world of insiders: EU officials, intellectuals, and political elites and those interest and pressure groups who functioned at European levels. The Convention did not solve the EU's broader problem of communicating beyond such insiders—in fact it deepened the problem.

The Constitution proposed a number of institutional changes to cope with enlargement—in particular changes in the composition of the European Commission. It also proposed new powers for the European Parliament, and a new approach to weighting national votes in the European Council (the so-called "dual majority" procedure—of states and of populations—that better reflected the relative sizes of member states). These changes were really matters of institutional tinkering and did not create a great deal of elite conflict, even though they caused apprehension among smaller member states, afraid of domination by larger ones.

There were also a few broader proposals, like those for a longer-term Council president and a foreign minister, intended to enhance the capacity of the EU to represent its interests externally and speak more-or-less authoritatively with national counterparts. In addition, the Constitution included some slippery wording on moving from unanimity to qualified majority decision-making in certain areas. In general, however, the proposed Constitution was remarkable for its lack of bold new initiatives.

In its first two parts, the Constitution presented the European Union in simple and persuasive ways. Part One, which was a readable fifteen pages, set out the core values and objectives of the European Union in terms that had broad appeal. Among other things, Europe was for peace and freedom, against poverty, social exclusion and discrimination of all kinds. It was in favor of equality between men and women, solidarity between generations, and the protection of children. Europe stood for cohesion between its different regions, enhanced social protection and justice, and a competitive "social market economy." Part Two was a five-page Charter of Fundamental Rights, guaranteeing wide-ranging human, social, economic, and political rights. All well and good.

Had the Constitution ended after Part Two it might have been spared the indignities that the French and Dutch inflicted upon it. Alas, there was also Part Three, a long, detailed, and dense recapitulation of what the EU could do, and how it should do it institutionally. This made the Constitutional document into 200 pages, 448 articles, 36 protocols and 50 declarations. Part Three was necessary to integrate the EU's many previous treaties, but it added nothing useful and was full of references to liberalization and market building. It was read and denounced endlessly in France, the Netherlands, and elsewhere, even though it did little more than recapitulate the arcane details of fifty years of integration.

Unfortunately for the success of the Constitution, European citizens were asked to consider the Constitution at the worst possible time. Economies were in the dumps. Unemployment was painfully high. The European social and economic models—which promised extensive social protections—were under assault from all sides. A proposed directive from the Commission for liberating the market for services was being portrayed as a threat to health care, as well as national controls over professional certification for private services. Thus the fictitious "Polish plumber" became an important symbol, underlining deep fears that immigrants from the new Eastern and Central European member states would swamp the EU-15. The prospect of Turkish accession to the EU, which was widely opposed, provided another red flag, provoking fears and mobilizing opposition to the Constitution.

In retrospect, the politics of the EU Constitution seem to confirm the famous maxim offered by Tip O'Neill, the former Speaker of the House, that "all politics is local." As we turn to our country-by-country analysis it becomes clear that the broad themes identified above are in play in every national context but—no surprise! — each case reveals a unique relationship between national and EU factors.

Britain

Tony Blair has been prime minister since 1997 and from the start he was determined to resolve Britain's ambivalence about Europe, heal the wounds left by Margaret Thatcher's stridently unit-Europe posture, and maximize British influence both within the EU and as an honest broker between America and Europe.

In some areas Britain has achieved considerable influence in Europe. Tony Blair's Britain preaches a globalization-friendly model of flexible labor markets throughout EU Europe, and its success in boosting Britain's economic performance in comparison with the rest of Europe has won some reluctant admirers, even converts. (For example, Chancellor Gerhard Schröder's economic reform package, Project 2010, has much in common with Blair's approach to economic governance that blends neoliberalism with pay-as-you-go social expenditures).

Britain has also played a leading role within the EU in advancing common foreign, security, and defense initiatives. Britain led Europe in the war in Kosovo, which Blair viewed as a critical test case for his commitment to apply diplomacy backed by force to prevent or contain humanitarian catastrophes. More generally, the ethical approach to foreign policy articulated by Blair and his first foreign secretary, Robin Cook—to make Britain "a leading force for good in the world"—resonated deeply in much of EU Europe.

Unfortunately, Blair's decision to "stand shoulder to shoulder" with President Bush when the post-9/11 war on terror moved from Afghanistan to Iraq embittered Britain's relationships with France and Germany (which strenuously opposed the war), and has vastly complicated Britain's ability to influence the economic reform and common foreign and security policies that have topped its EU agenda.

What about the euro and the Constitution? These issues have really taken a back seat in Britain. (In the May 2005 general election Europe was all but invisible). Blair promised a referendum to decide on whether Britain should adopt the euro but has conceded to the demands of his finance minister, Gordon Brown, that the decision will be based on a series of economic tests—and the date keeps slipping. With Blair's political capital depleted by the war in Iraq, Blair suddenly announced in April 2004 that Britain would hold a referendum on the Constitution. It was one thing, apparently, to ram an unpopular war through parliament, quite another to risk pushing through the EU Constitution!

As the French and Dutch votes approached, everyone assumed that Blair was hoping for a "no" vote before a UK vote, so the UK could not be blamed. And defeat in the UK was almost a forgone conclusion. Ladbrokes, the famous British bookmakers who take bets on almost anything, placed the odds for passage of the EU Constitution in Britain at 8:1 against!

In the end, even the French and Dutch defeats didn't save Britain in general—and Blair in particular—from the wrath of Schröder and Chirac, if not directly for the Constitution, then for defiantly demanding that agricultural subsidies and Britain's rebate be joined at the hip in budget negotiations.

Having limped to re-election in May 2005, Blair has promised not to run again and is expected to step down as prime minister at some point in the next few years in favor of his heir-apparent Gordon Brown. But he will have one final opportunity to achieve a positive legacy on Europe. The UK assumes the rotating presidency of the EU for a six-month term beginning in July 2005. While Blair remains Europe's favorite scapegoat—for advancing an economic and social model that challenges European social protection traditions and demanding reform of CAP—Britain insists that it will use its EU presidency to heal the rifts and unveil a new agenda to spur growth and trade as the way out of a sluggish economy in Europe. Even Ladbrokes may not want to cover that bet.

France

How can one explain the resounding French "non"? The majority opposed to the treaty might be considered the product of a perfect storm that comprised three elements: (1) the interactive effects of European integration and French economic malaise; (2) the very strong opposition of the most vulnerable; and (3) partisan politics.

When voters entered the voting booth to cast a ballot in the referendum, were they thinking primarily about the European Constitution or about the economy? According to exit polls, nearly half of "non" voters stated that they opposed the treaty because it would produce an increase in France's already high unemployment rate. The next reason most frequently cited by opponents of the treaty was that they were fed up with the entire situation in France. About a third of the no voters opposed the treaty because of its neoliberal agenda. They believed it would shred France's extensive social safety net, including generous pensions, high minimum wages, and extensive health and unemployment insurance benefits. And a third of the opponents said they opposed the treaty because it was too complicated. (Respondents were permitted to offer more than one rationale for their votes). Of course—and this is the critical point—since France's economic difficulties began to increase in the 1980s, just as economic integration was gaining momentum, voters had every reason to link Europe's future and the French economy. In effect, a "non" was a rejection of both.

This perspective was especially powerful among the most economically vulnerable: those most in danger of losing their jobs, who opposed the treaty. An astonishingly high 81 percent of manual workers and 60 percent of lower middle class voters opposed the treaty. Thus, the EU referendum pitted a more prosperous, economically secure France against a France more fearful of the increased insecurity a stronger EU would produce.

Finally, partisan politics was very much in play in the French "non." Most parties on the far left of the political spectrum opposed the referendum (as did the

National Front on the xenophobic right). The Socialist Party (PS), however, one of France's three major governing parties and a traditional supporter of the EU, was much more divided. After three-fifths of Socialist party members voted for a yes vote in the party's own internal referendum in late 2004, most party leaders lobbied hard for this outcome in the referendum campaign itself. However, several prominent PS leaders, including Laurent Fabius, a former prime minister, joined most of the fringe left parties in opposing the referendum. This division among the party leadership--and Socialists' hostility to Chirac—led to a "non" vote by 59 percent of PS sympathizers. This was enough to defeat the Constitution.

The outcome of the referendum was a bombshell, perhaps second only to the 2002 presidential election, in which Jean-Marie Le Pen, a far-right candidate scored an astonishing breakthrough. It symbolized the determination of a majority of French to question the judgment of mainstream politicians. The biggest losers were these politicians—especially President Jacques Chirac, along with his political allies, and Socialist Party leaders. President Chirac immediately became a lame duck president. The second casualty of the referendum was Chirac's handpicked prime minister, Jean-Pierre Raffarin. Dominique de Villepin, another ally of Chirac and a potential contender in the 2007 presidential election, replaced him. A third casualty of the referendum was Chirac's ruling party, the Union pour un Mouvement Populaire (UMP), which campaigned for a "oui" vote and was tarnished by the rejection of the referendum.

Leaders of the PS, the major opposition party, could take little comfort from the humiliation suffered by the leaders of the government and ruling party. For the PS also campaigned in favor of the referendum and shared responsibility for its defeat. After the defeat, top party leaders swiftly voted to remove Fabius from his leadership position. But the PS was in shambles and faced an immense challenge preparing for the 2007 presidential elections.

Germany

In May 2005, with 569 yes votes, 23 no votes and two abstentions, the German Bundestag approved the new European Union Constitution, but the situation is more complicated than this vote might suggest.

Germans want the EU, but not this EU. Most Germans would like to try to find a way to resuscitate the social market economy. This is made all the more difficult by a Social Democratic Party that is marching resolutely to the right, as evidenced by the Agenda 2010 and the Hartz IV reforms that are gutting the heart of what the social market economy was. The fact that this departure is being led by Social Democratic Chancellor Schröder is even more bizarre, since he has a constituency that actually likes and wants the kind of social protection that they used to have. The problem is that nobody has any idea how to get it.

There are three big exogenous problems and one big endogenous one.

First, a high everything model of ever higher skills producing ever higher-quality products may be finally meeting its match because the newly industrializing countries, particularly India and China, can catch up too fast. German firms do not have a very good answer for this, other than going offshore to places that pay lower wages and may or may not have the quality of labor that they need. Despite this challenge there is still a tremendous amount of human capital that remains, but is not being effectively tapped.

Second, the costs of German unification have been a huge drag on the capacity of the organized capitalist model to regain competitiveness. Economic stagnation will likely continue for the better part of the next decade. This has produced in its wake a revival of the PDS, the renamed eastern German Communist Party, and the beginnings of right wing movements that are for the moment still considerably smaller than similar right-wing movements in other European countries.

Third, the institutional architecture of the EU is the antithesis of the old social market economy model, which involved a coordinated set of institutions working with market sector actors in ways that fostered relationships not deals and produced high economic growth, high living standards, and considerable labor market and political peace. However, the current regime of economic liberalism combined with restrictive monetary policy and a 3 percent fiscal straitjacket (that only now is beginning to be ignored) is the antithesis of what the German model used to be about. The larger point is that markets move much faster than institutions and it takes time to establish institutions when you have a new market reality. The question of the day is whether or not Germans can resuscitate a revised set of institutions to deal with the new reality because Germans are very ineffective at economic liberalization and free market policies.

The large endogenous problem is that Germans have lost their institutional memory. In the past 15 years the ability to develop innovative ideas to adapt their organized capitalist social market economy to economic challenges has atrophied. Most policymakers have reflexively based their responses to these challenges on old prevailing practices and not on a purposeful response to specific contemporary challenges. It is quite unclear whether Germany can find a 21st century version of its once redoubtable institutional model. Much about the fate of Germany and the future of the EU hangs in the balance.

Italy

The referendums in France and the Netherlands fell in a very tumultuous political period in Italy. The economy has been reeling, producing fierce criticism from practically the entire economic spectrum (including Confindustria, the main business organization, which has effectively disowned Prime Minister Silvio Berlusconi), as well as from the European Central Bank. This stagnation was, in turn, largely responsible for the severe defeat of the governing coalition in regional elections in April 2005, which saw 10 of 12 regions won by the Center-Left opposition.

At the same time, the referendums on Europe overlapped with a contentious Italian referendum in June on various human reproductive issues, which hogged much of the headlines and political air space. Divisions between observant Catholics and more secular Italians, and discussions of the resurgence of the Church in the aftermath of the death of Pope John Paul II, tended to push the discussion of Europe into the background.

Italy has always been, and remains, one of the most strongly pro-European countries. The Constitution was passed overwhelmingly by the Italian

Parliament. The vote was 436-28 in the Chamber (in January 2005) and 217-16 in the Senate (in April). The main open opposition came from the Northern League on the right, and from Rifondazione Comunista on the left. There were also dissenters from the left wing of the DS (Left Democrats, the main opposition party) and from within Berlusconi's own Forza Italia. The strength of Italy's pro-European consensus is evident in the fact that most opponents chose not to show up in Parliament when the Constitution was voted, rather than make a public show of their disagreement.

On the social level, even the most left wing union confederation, the CGIL, supported the idea of European unity, although it framed its support in terms of defending and expanding a distinctly European welfare state, while opposing the imposition of neoliberal cutbacks and austerity. The CGIL's left wing opposed the Constitution. Among business interests, export-oriented producers and service providers were quite enthusiastic, while smaller, more vulnerable producers showed concern about, if not outright fear of, competition that might threaten their security. But it remains striking how much lip-service continues to be paid to the idea of "Europe". So almost everyone (except the Northern League) was at pains to insist that "Europe" had not been defeated, but only a particular version of Europe: the Europe of far-off, insensitive bureaucrats or those who listened to the banks and not to the people.

This argument was made with special glee by the Euroskeptical elements in Forza Italia, as well as other members of Berlusconi's coalition. Why? Genuine skeptics were happy to see "Europe" get a black eye. But for many others, this was a way to link Romano Prodi to what had been rejected. He had, after all, been the President of the European Commission for five years, and he is almost certain to lead the Center-Left in the scheduled 2006 general election. So, for political opponents, anything that hurts him is a good thing. Meanwhile, Berlusconi, while trying not to disavow European unity altogether, wants to avoid any association with the belt-tightening (and increased tax collection) associated with the Prodi years.

The longer-term response to Europe's future will depend to a large extent on the nature of Italy's recent economic problems. The most pessimistic

Copyright © Houghton Mifflin Company. All rights reserved.

interpretations emphasize that the very sectors in which Italy's dynamic small firms—which have accounted for so much of its growth in recent years—are strongest (textiles, leather goods, niche manufacturing) are now profoundly threatened by foreign competition. Even if these negative scenarios are somewhat exaggerated (Gucci and Prada probably have little to fear from the Chinese), there is certainly considerable truth in these observations. It is also the case that the Italians have perennially spent less on research and development than have other major European countries, and even they are under increasing economic pressure. These difficulties help explain the apparent flip-flopping about Europe from even such a traditionally staunch supporter as Italy. The longer the slump continues, the more complex the situation will be, irrespective of which coalition is in power.

East-Central Europe

The French and Dutch rejection of the EU Constitution came as a shock to the newest members in East-Central Europe: for some a pleasant shock, for others a most unwelcome one. "We were supposed to be the ones upset about integration happening so fast, not them," one Polish sociologist wrote to us after the recent events. She was referring to the recent talk about the EU being dominated by a "core Europe" in the west, with the new members consigned to second-class citizenship. These suspicions had led to growing Euroskepticism in the region after the 2004 enlargement, which the proposed Constitution had amplified.

In Poland, by far the largest of the new members, critics pointed to the Constitution's new EU voting procedures, less favorable to Poland than the Nice Treaty it would have replaced, and to the fact that the more secular western countries were unwilling to put into the Constitution a preamble stressing Europe's Christian traditions, an important issue for Catholic Poland. Many leading politicians in the Czech Republic also criticized the Constitution for what they saw as its overly centralizing design.

Yet East European critics were in a pickle: they didn't want to be the ones to bring the Constitution down, since they knew westerners would see this as ingratitude, and because the EU had in fact brought economic benefits, particularly in Poland. What they hoped for is that others would turn it down first – and these people got their wishes. Or sort of: for they are not pleased that one of the reasons the French and Dutch rejected the Constitution was their own displeasure at the perceived costs of eastward expansion. Indeed, in their drive to get out the vote, as we have seen, French foes of the Constitution popularized a stereotypical "Polish plumber" allegedly taking the jobs of French citizens (even though there are only 8000 registered Polish workers in all of France!) And sure enough, the EU budget conference held soon after the French vote refused to grant the new members the levels of financial assistance they were expecting. This is exactly what East European proponents of the Constitution had feared.

What happens in light of the vote in France and the Netherlands? There are two views – particularly important for the only two eastern countries, Poland and the Czech Republic, where referendums on the issue had been scheduled. (In Hungary and Slovakia, like Latvia, Lithuania, and Slovenia, parliament ratified the Constitution before the rejection crisis; Estonia probably still will.) One view says that the crisis opens up a special opportunity for these countries to be shapers of the new EU, rather than its junior partners, provided the countries hold the referendums and pass it. As Poland's outgoing prime minister put it, by showing our commitment to Europe precisely at a time when some in the West are skeptical, we can become one of the acknowledged leaders in helping resolve the impasse. The governing Social Democratic Party in the Czech Republic agrees, adding that choosing not to hold the referendum now would be a sign of acknowledging its own unimportance, not a good position to take for a country trying to prove its legitimacy.

Critics, however, say that the Constitution is already dead – thankfully – and that the British decision to postpone a referendum demonstrates that canceling the referendum is not a sign of weakness. They say that the task now is to articulate an alternative vision of Europe, without the western focus or tendencies to centralization.

In the end, most East European populations still support the EU, across age, class, and regional divides, and few of them see any alternative. Their chief fear – being treated as second-class citizens – is what allows politicians to score points by scolding the EU, even as they moderate these positions once they come to power. But the French and Dutch voters may have done the new members a favor, by showing them that they were not the only ones with reservations about the Constitution, and by eliminating the specter of a western "core" committed to centralization. In this sense, the present crisis can well lay the grounds for a more legitimate, inclusive, and consensual political union in the future.

Where will the EU go from here?

EU cynics are having a field day. It's the economy, stupid. It's the lack of democracy and transparency. It's global competitive pressures and neoliberalism chipping away at the European social and economic model. It's the distant, arrogant, and aloof European bureaucrats—or the national politicians who are no better!

National leaders have played a deceptive two-level game—and have finally been caught! They have been using Europe as a lever to create EU-level programs that oblige their constituencies to undergo reforms—mainly cuts in social protections— which they would never have permitted at the national level. In the end, the no votes delivered a simple message to the political elites: You can try to fool the people all the time, but it won't work, especially if you call referendums to ask them how they feel about being fooled!

There is an old maxim about sports, "Your team is never as good as it looks when you are winning—or as bad as it looks when you are losing." For now, the EU looks pretty bad, but it is worth remembering its extraordinary record of achievements.

Against the horrifying backdrop of World War II, the founders of the European Coal and Steel Community (1950) and then the European Economic Community (1958) calculated that promoting economic cooperation would enable member countries to bury past differences and become political allies. For half a century—and despite some important bumps in the road—the plan has worked brilliantly, contributing significantly to stability, peace, and prosperity for the member states.

The "non" votes in May-June 2005 were a very significant setback for the EU, signaling, above all, that the Union is likely to remain stuck in place for a number of years. For the foreseeable future, it will be very difficult to achieve intergovernmental consent on movement forward in foreign policy and defense, on the budget, on enlargement.

The EU's future, however, will largely be determined by what key member states do about their domestic problems. And on this, the effect of the Constitution should not be exaggerated. Even had France provided a reverberating "oui", it would not have been easy to reform the European "social model" to spur more growth and greater competitiveness without destroying all that is unique and good about Europe, starting with the economic security and social solidarities that Europeans demand.

The defeat of the Constitution makes solving these problems more difficult. But it should not—and must not—justify inertia or extreme pessimism. After all, it is just possible that the period of turmoil and reflection that the no votes inspired will provoke some hard thinking and productive political mobilizations to revitalize the Union, narrow the gap between citizens and elites, and resolve the institutional and programmatic challenges of enlargement and competitiveness.